Mark Wheeller

Missing Dan Nolan

A Verbatim Play

Salamander Street

PLAYS

Dan Nolan - Missing first published by dbda in 2003 (978190284310X);
Missing Dan Nolan published by dbda in 2004 (9781902843162); Published in
a new edition by Zinc Communicate in 2020 ISBN 978 1 902843 46 9

This edition first published in 2020 by Salamander Street Ltd., 272 Bath Street,
Glasgow, G2 4JR (info@salamanderstreet.com)

Missing Dan Nolan © Mark Wheeller, 2003-2008

Photograph appears with kind permission of Daniel Nolan's family.

PB ISBN: 9781913630287
E ISBN: 9781913630294

Cover and text design by Konstantinos Vasdekis

10 9 8 7 6 5 4 3 2 1

Further copies of this publication can be purchased from
www.salamanderstreet.com

CONTENTS

Acknowledgements

Pauline, Greg and Clare Nolan; DSI Stewart (Hampshire Police); "Andy", George, "Jo", Sarah, "Thom" and their families, for giving me their words and permission to re-tell this story.

The cast of the Oaklands Youth Theatre production 2002/3.

Sophie Gorell Barnes and all at MBA for their continued support and belief.

Thanks to dbda (later known as Zinc Publishing) who originally made this play available to schools when others would not have done so.

Thanks to George Spender and those in the Salamander Street team for their efforts to extend the reach of my plays.

My wife, Rachel, and children (Ollie, Charlie & Daisy) for love and support… and tolerance of long working hours.

Roy Nevitt (Stantonbury Campus) in the early eighties for his inspiration in the use of documentary theatre… "Dig where you stand".

Whoever performs this play must not lose sight of the fact that it tells a true story in the words of those most closely involved. Words must not be changed. Edits should not be made for public performances without permission.

Agreement was gained from all parties who contributed to the play on the understanding that this would be the version performed. Even in private showings, any cuts should be made with due sensitivity to the real people from the tragedy.

All performing groups must respect the willingness of the various families to allow their words to be used in the way that they appear in this published text.

Introduction

Written for the first published version of the play (with a few corrections) when it was called *Dan Nolan – Missing*.

- The National Missing Persons Helpline receives more than 100,000 calls every year!!!
- It helps to resolve 70% of the cases it works on.
- 30% remain tragically unresolved.

These were the shocking statistics that confronted me when I approached a stand surrounded by "Dan Nolan MISSING" posters outside Tesco in April 2002.

I had originally seen posters announcing Dan's disappearance early in January while walking my dogs. I continued to see them but, as there had been nothing on the television about him, I assumed that he had been found or perhaps he was not missing after all. As I came to realise that he was still missing it seemed apparent to me that society considered Dan's disappearance to be less important... less serious... or more likely to be resolved quickly than the ones I heard about in the media. I could not understand the situation, so out of curiosity as to how a stall outside Tesco could help, I approached the stall holders to discover that they were trying to raise awareness. They had found it very difficult to get any ongoing media coverage. As a parent (of three) myself, I was shocked.

I put myself in their position... how would I feel if my son or daughter went missing and I was not able to convey this fact to the public at large through the media? I realised, I may be able to help.

To cut a long story short, I offered to write a dramatic reconstruction (also raising any other issues Dan's story might throw up). I approached four Oaklands Youth Theatre members to become committed to such a project in our own time. It was crucial to get "the show on the road" to help Dan's parents in their quest for more coverage as soon as possible. First, I had a period of research…

As I came within a mile of the Nolans' family home in Hamble for my first interview, I couldn't help but see posters plastered to every one of the thirty or forty trees and lamp posts… the blow-ups of the posters gradually getting bigger. This clearly communicated the impression of a very loving family on a determined, if not desperate, search for a much-loved son.

One of the first things I saw as I went into the Nolans' house to do my first interview, was "that photo" I'd seen of Dan in the missing posters, in its original school photo style frame… the way it was meant to be seen. It gave that photo, in its original setting, an added poignancy. I remembered my own school photos that I had wanted to hide from other people… and wondered what Dan had thought of this one, little knowing how well known it was destined to become.

Immediately, I realised that the documentary style of writing I had used for *Too Much Punch for Judy* and *Graham* was the way I wanted to approach this play. It was crucial to convey the facts and opinions in the way that the people who had experienced this situation first hand phrased it. Consequently, *Dan Nolan – Missing* uses the words of Daniel's family, friends (some of whom were with him that night) and the detective in charge of the ongoing investigation, to try and get as close to the truth as memory will allow.

On interviewing the friends who shared that fateful evening with Dan, I was struck by their youth. They were, like I imagine Dan, "normal" fourteen/fifteen-year-old boys.

This tragic story was initially performed by a small group from the Oaklands Youth Theatre who were of a similar age to Daniel Nolan. I believe it can be performed between anyone from the age of fourteen and fifty.

Whoever performs this play must not lose sight of the fact that it tells a true story in the words of those most closely involved. Words must not be changed. Edits should not be made for public performances without permission. Agreement was gained from all parties who contributed to the play on the understanding that this would be the version performed. Even in private showings, any cuts should be made with due sensitivity to the real people from the tragedy.

All performing groups must respect the willingness of the various families to allow their words to be used in the way that they appear in this published text.

I have slightly developed what I wrote in my original introduction for *Hard to Swallow*. It is equally pertinent for *Dan Nolan – Missing*.

It must at all times be remembered when reading or performing this play that the events portrayed are as close to the truth as memory will allow. The performers should not impersonate the real-life characters (it is unlikely that they will know them to be able to do so). They should breathe into them a life that is a reasonable interpretation of the words in the script as honestly and truthfully as the performer can manage. Unless specifically instructed to do otherwise for a particular effect, the actors should avoid overstatement and veer towards underplaying. Trust the material. It is, after all, as near as possible the "real" thing.

The other thing to add here is to say that with all my documentary/verbatim plays there are often long speeches. It is crucial that these are not all static. The director should try to be imaginative and animate the scene to keep the visual interest for the audience as high as possible without detracting from the power of the "real" words.

All of us who were involved in the first production of the play have become passionately involved with the subject matter and hope that our efforts and those of other groups who also choose to present this play may help to solve the mystery of Dan's disappearance.

The school photo of Dan Nolan as used in so many of the posters the family had distributed in their 'Missing' campaign.

Afterword by Mark Wheeller

Written for the first publication of Missing Dan Nolan,
(as opposed to Dan Nolan – Missing) March 2004.

It is now just over two years since Dan's tragic disappearance. Much has happened in that time... but the news for Dan's family is not good. All their (and our) hopes of Dan returning home seem to have been dashed as remains of a foot, found last year on a remote beach in Swanage, were identified as Dan's. This version of the play has been updated to account for these tragic developments... but Dan's family and friends remain supportive of all the play can continue to do.

"Although we've lost our Dan, I feel very proud.
All the issues about Dan's disappearance and the safety issues surrounding
teenagers are in the play and it must continue to raise awareness."
Pauline Nolan

The Oaklands Youth Theatre continued to perform the play in various places until October 2003. The cast have all moved on to other things now... but this period in all our lives will remain clear in our collective memories as a time where we did something that could help and support the Nolan family in their time of need. Each performance we did was updated (with new lines for the committed cast to learn for each and every performance) with the new information as it came to light.

The cast who performed those initial productions enabled me, not only to update the story, but to experiment with the structure of the way I presented the play. They, in turn, became involved in a production that won numerous awards and gave them huge confidence in their ability in the performing arts. The motivation of performing this true story in front of those who had lived through it could never have been greater and, I believe, led them to perform to a higher standard than any other sort of production could have ever achieved. For me this is one of the main reasons I have found verbatim theatre to be such a force for student theatre performances.

All are wanting to go on to further their careers in this field.

Missing Dan Nolan is not only a slightly different title, but is a much tighter script. I will continue to add updates to my website (and future editions) if they occur… but the basic structure will now remain in place. It is, I believe, an important play which is very accessible for teenagers as it concerns them so directly. More schools than I could ever have hoped for have adopted it as a study or performance text. It has only been available for a year and its immediate popularity has led to this new edition being printed. I hope that it goes on to spread its wings even further to provide a long lasting and fitting testament to Dan Nolan's all too brief life.

Afterword to the 2020 Edition by Mark Wheeller

We were all aware we were involved in a very *special* production, but none of us could ever have imagined how well-known this play would become.

Oaklands Youth Theatre/Community School (knocked down in 2014) in the very unspectacular area of Lordshill in Southampton. It was no Winchester College, but we had a professionally equipped theatre. In terms of our Youth Theatre, I set our aims high. My first original production was selected to be showcased at the Royal National Theatre. In the ensuing years we were selected to perform at the National Student Drama Festival, mostly populated by university and drama school productions. When I announced any new Youth Theatre production I supposed the potential members were vaguely aware of our track record. Regardless, they were aware that if they volunteered to become involved they would be working *very* hard (for the fun of doing it seriously).

I approached Darren, Rachael, Alex and Kate (with my friend and ex-student Danny Sturrock offering technical assistance) because I knew from their work, either in curriculum time or Youth Theatre, that they would be totally committed, so much so that they chose to give up much of their summer holiday to make the production happen. I didn't have to motivate them to give their best. Once they heard what the production was they leapt onboard and did just that. It *really* mattered to us all.

We all had to get it right. That meant hard work.

We had zero budget, so had to get the play up and running with very limited resources. Danny had the bright idea of painting four of the theatre's cubes to offer a thematic colour, using a sea blue that would give an impression of waves – a whole set for the cost of a couple of cans of paint! We used these cubes in various different arrangements to show the many different locations of the play. They also offered us the ability to have different levels. On top of that we had the ongoing cost of candles and Tesco

Finest Chocolate Truffle Cake. The Nolan family donated one of their huge posters, the same one I had seen on the day I travelled to Hamble for the first time, to act as our backdrop. We also bought T-shirts with the missing poster emblazoned onto them. We did the whole thing for well under £50.

Our focus was twofold: that the production would lead to news of Dan for his family and that we would create a committed piece of theatre that would attract a large audience. We hoped people would be impressed with the way we told this story. With the huge amount of narration we had to be imaginative in finding movement to illustrate the words being spoken, whilst also making every speech visually arresting. There was only one part where we needed help – the opening section, which we wanted to arrest the audience's attention instantly. I invited an ex-student of mine in to help. Matt Kane had made a career from directing the professional touring productions of both *Too Much Punch For Judy* & *Legal Weapon II*, so I was keeping it 'in the family'. He generated a high energy start that we never needed to alter. Thanks, Matt!

Schools tell me the only way to attract a decent audience was to do large-scale musicals. We trod a different path. We wanted to tell real stories *about* our community, *to* our community. We had no problem selling out frequently and created such a buzz around the town that we were featured on TV news programmes several times. This was *our* way of making a successful production. It worked.

None of us could have predicted what this so-called small production would go on to achieve in the years to come.

I admit that from the outset I had hopes that it would be toured into schools professionally. This had happened to a number of my previous plays, so seemed well within reach. This is precisely why I chose to work with a cast of four (2m 2f), so that it would be suitable for a professional TIE company. I hoped some of the cast would go on to become part of these professional companies.

In this respect, *Missing Dan Nolan* has underachieved. It only toured once, in 2006 by the Queen's Theatre Hornchurch in that small region. It was a great production so I have no idea why it didn't continue.

In 2016, a director who had successfully taken my *Graham – World's Fastest Blind Runner* to the Edinburgh Fringe put on a large cast Youth Theatre production at the Lichfield Garrick Theatre where he had recently been appointed Artistic Director. It was a stunning production and features on the (current as I write) Wheellerplays DVD of the play which is now shown in schools alongside our original OYT production. Tim's was very different to our four person TIE version and used the ensemble imaginatively adding a new and exciting dimension to the production.

What was also notable about that production was that Dan's sister, Clare attended. Clare was probably thirteen when I met and interviewed her. The interview happened as an afterthought quite spontaneously when Clare wandered into the room. I was interviewing Pauline and she asked Clare if she wanted to speak. I remember Clare's eloquence and her poignant memories of this massive tragedy. I drove back home afterwards, thinking how it would have been a great idea to do the whole play from Clare's perspective, especially given that the performers would, as Youth Theatre members, be young people but, I felt it would be inappropriate to put her under such pressure so took the thought no further. (It's only recently that I spoke to Clare about my thoughts on that day.)

Clare attended the OYT performances and was always chatty afterwards and, a few years later I was pleased to become Facebook friends. We messaged one another when something newsworthy happened with the play. One of these messages was about the Lichfield performance and I let her know that, despite the distance, I was planning to attend. Clare and her boyfriend decided they would attend and she agreed to be part of a Q&A with the cast after the performance.

It was wonderful meeting her after such a long break and, having seen the production the previous evening, I knew the performance was a stunner! She was duly blown away by it. Her contribution to the Q&A afterwards floored me. The passion with which she spoke about how her brother's disappearance wasn't a simple case of drowning… she was certain there were far more sinister motives behind his disappearance.

There was another moment in 2016, where I remember messaging Clare, a moment where the play overreached any expectations I could ever have had for any of my plays produced for a Youth Theatre in a school on an unexceptional estate in Southampton.

In 2016 OCR examination board announced that *Missing Dan Nolan* was to become a set text for the new GCSE (9-1) Drama examination alongside plays that came out of the professional world of theatre. I hadn't been contacted to forewarn me of this so it came as a total surprise!

When it was first studied there was some debate about whether they should study the OYT production or the subsequent professional tour. I was adamant that it should be OYT, as this is where the real development of the play had occurred. That was where the story was – the story of us performing it in *our* theatre and getting the most incredible review when we first performed it:

I can't remember the last time I saw a grown man, a stranger, cry in front of me. Or, for that matter, sat in a room of people gripped by mutual sorrow and unspeakable heartache.

This play about the tragic evening that the fifteen-year-old Hamble boy went missing after a fishing trip with friends will haunt everyone who witnesses it.

It's a gripping human drama that will appeal to – and appall – anyone with a heart.

As the tale of a family in freefall unfolded, slowly and silently loved ones sought out each others' hands and clasped them tightly in the darkness to a chorus of staccato sniffs and muffled sobs.

A row of young lads were trying desperately to hide their embarrassed tears in front of their mates – who wouldn't have noticed anyway because they too were sobbing.

Also in the audience, the play's central characters – Dan's mum, Pauline Nolan and her daughter Clare – watched themselves portrayed by the young amateur thespians from Oaklands Youth Theatre.

The performance is based on real conversations with the family and instead of a script there has been an editing process where their statements have been fused into a coherent and powerful dialogue.

Dan's last known movements are brought to life as well as the events leading up to and just after his disappearance at Hamble Quay on New Year's Day.

It raises questions of the police who appeared slow to act. It took them a week to print missing posters, CCTV footage from the village was only analysed after the family prompted and key information took months to uncover because witnesses were not thoroughly quizzed.

The overriding impression from the play is that the police assumed the worst had happened to Dan and were not prepared to put resources into a manhunt.

But the family, it becomes clear, are adamant that their precious son and brother is still alive. Throughout the play they press a disturbing case that all avenues have not been explored.

Every person who has fallen into the Hamble and drowned has had their body recovered. The longest it has taken for a body to surface is four months.

Dan went missing eleven months ago.

Ben Clerkin, *Southern Evening Echo*

We took it to our local Totton Drama Festival, fully expecting to win, so much so that we didn't even rehearse in the week of the festival. We ended up coming second to last! The cast were pulled up for their poor diction, something I viewed as just a fact of "Lordshill kids" and the structure of the play was questioned and new suggestions offered.

Rather than returning home and falling apart I re-wrote the script, using the suggestions of the knowledgeable adjudicator. The cast came in, rehearsed hard and frequently, determined to improve their enunciation. Six months later we took our refined production to the Woking Drama Festival (the biggest amateur One-Act Drama Festival in the country and...

... WE WON THE YOUTH AWARD!!!

It wasn't easy. But we did it − by working relentlessly and overcoming any problems that confronted us. There was never any mention of the cast's words being indistinct for *any* OYT show from that point onwards.

One of the most wonderful things I can say about this production is that the cast and crew remain in touch (partly due to Facebook), are still very proud of what we achieved together and now, nearly twenty years on, aware that the early production is studied. I am pleased (for the first time) to bring their memories to you as well as mine...

I hope you find the play as fulfilling as we did. Please try to bring something new to it just as we had to.

A Note from Pauline Nolan

Written in December 2002, one year after Dan had disappeared,
immediately prior to the first edition being printed,
and prior to the discovery at Swanage.

We have watched those desperate appeals on TV by
parents whose children have gone missing, so many
times it seems. "What a terrible situation, we could
never cope if we lost one of our children!"

All natural reactions, never believing that we would
ever be in this situation – but, here we are. Never
believing that out of our five children it would happen
to Dan, but it has.

Nobody is invincible. Life is very fragile. This can
happen to anybody irrespective of class, nationality,
religion or location. It is devastating to the friends
and families who have to deal with a loved one being
missing, the not knowing! We need to know where Dan
is and this is why we were happy for Mark to write
Dan's story in the form of this play.

We hope for two things: Firstly that the play will be
seen by somebody who may have that vital missing
link regarding Dan, therefore allowing us to locate
his whereabouts. Secondly, to try and find something
constructive from every parent's worst nightmare.
We believe that all things happen for a reason. Maybe
this is why Dan has gone missing?

We don't want anybody to feel how we are feeling.

We need to try to make a difference.

Pauline Nolan

Dan Nolan – Missing premiered by the Oaklands Youth Theatre at Oaklands Community School Theatre on Saturday 23rd November 2002 with the following cast:

Pauline Nolan/Joe	Kate Dean
Dan Nolan/DSI Stewart/Andy	Darren Harley
Greg Nolan/George	Alex Chalk
Clare Nolan/Thom/Sarah	Rachael Dennett
Director	Mark Wheeller
Assistant Director & Lighting Designer	Danny Sturrock
Sound	Ollie Wheeller/Laura Clarke
Photography/slides	Mark (Sparky) Harbord
Live Music	Arjun Malhotra/Charlie Wheeller

Missing Dan Nolan was first presented by the same cast at the Woking Drama Festival on Friday 10th October 2003. It was awarded the Woking Drama Festival Youth Award for the best play by a cast under 21. You can read parts of the report by the adjudicator Paul Fowler GODA, on pages 48-49.

Productions of *Missing Dan Nolan* should use minimal props, costumes *(with the exception of Dan who was kitted out in duplicate clothing)* and setting so that the play can be performed without a break. There should be no blackouts and scene changes should be incorporated into the scenes or underscored with pre-recorded music.

Characters

The play was originally written for four actors although there are many more characters than that.

Missing Dan Nolan can be performed by any number from 4 (2m/2f) to 14 (9m, 4f, 1 m/f).

Cast list in order of appearance:

DAN NOLAN
Fourteen years old. Needs to be dressed in a grey
"Benny" hat and beige Henri Lloyd jacket…
with blue trousers.

GEORGE
Fourteen years old

THOM
Fifteen years old

JOE
Fourteen years old

CLARE NOLAN
Dan's younger sister. Thirteen years old.

PAULINE NOLAN
Dan's mother

GREG NOLAN
Dan's father

LIAM NOLAN
Dan's brother (in the dog poo scene)

SARAH
Dan's school friend

MAX
Dan's school friend

LORNA
Dan's school friend

ANDY
Thom's father

POLICE LIAISON OFFICER
As remembered by Pauline

DSI STEWART
Detective Superintendent in charge of the investigation

When performed by a cast of 2m & 2f the roles could be distributed as follows:

M1
Dan Nolan, PLO, Andy, DSI Stewart

M2
Greg, Liam, Max, George

F1
Pauline, Lorna, Joe

F2
Clare, Sarah, Thom

Section 1

MISSING DAN NOLAN

SL is a table on which the Truffle Cake will be put. On SR there is a small selection of musical instruments, used during the play.

Music 1: Silent Night *by* **Sinead O'Connor** *plays[1].*

THOM, JOE, GEORGE *and* **DAN** *enter and set up for some fishing. All are wearing clothes suitable for a cold night's fishing.* **DAN** *has a beige Henri Lloyd jacket, blue cotton trousers and Air Force blue DCs with the laces untied. The boys are lit as though by moonlight.*

DAN *(in slow motion) takes a vodka bottle from his backpack, unscrews it, then takes a swig. Music with a skate punk feel (Blink 182 – All The Small Things) segues seamlessly under the Sinead song.*

The three boys pass the bottle between themselves and, except **GEORGE**, *who refuses to drink, they each take swigs.* **THOM** *and* **JOE** *begin to mess around involving* **DAN** *and* **GEORGE** *in their japes, amongst other things they prank* **GEORGE**'s *mobile and laugh.* **GEORGE** *leaves without any fuss.*

JOE *and* **THOM** *continue to lark around energetically. Finally* **JOE** *is sick.* **THOM** *helps* **JOE** *home.* **DAN** *remains on his own. The lights crossfade to establish* **DAN**'s *home.* **DAN** *begins to "headbang".*

CLARE *enters angrily.*

CLARE: *(Shouting over the music.)* Turn it down, Dan!

DAN: *(Shouting over the music.)* What?

CLARE: *(Shouting over the music.)* Turn it down!

DAN: *(The music stops.)* That better is it?

CLARE: You're so selfish playing all that banging stuff so loud!

DAN: Well I'm out tonight so you can play "Westlife" up full and prance around as much as you like!

CLARE: We're a typical brother/sister… eighteen months apart. *(Laughing.)* We compete to see who can play the loudest music.

---

[1]   The songs/music suggested at various points in the play are suggestions only. They were used in the original production, after discussion with his family and tried to reflect Dan's taste in music and his Irish heritage. Please see prsformusic.com for copyright enquiries.

DAN: *(DAN is getting his stuff together to go out.)* No contest!

CLARE: He's got a better CD player than me so he always wins.

PAULINE: *(To the audience, contrastingly slow paced.)* I wake up every day thinking we could get some vital information. However, I realise it's probably just another day I've got to face.

CLARE: When I'm sitting by the door at school I play this game. I tell myself, if I look up the receptionist will be there to tell me my brother's returned home. It may be stupid but sometimes I do look up.

(CLARE exits.)

PAULINE: All the clairvoyants we spoke to in the weeks after Dan went missing said somebody took our Dan. One said he'll definitely come home. None said he fell in the water.

GREG: Many people believe our Dan went straight in the water... but that's not the only possibility...

PAULINE & GREG: ... not at all.

GREG: That river was searched...

PAULINE: ... every day...

GREG: ... on both tides... for three months.

PAULINE: All of the yachts there have been dived under... fingertip searches...

GREG: ... so if he'd've got trapped,

PAULINE & GREG: ... he would've been found.

GREG: Two large sonar units have been on the river... army sonar units...

PAULINE: ... and found nothing...

GREG: ... nothing. For Dan to go in the river that night...

PAULINE: ... to dodge every mooring line...

GREG: … every boat…

PAULINE: … to get into the main channel…

GREG: … to get out of the mouth of the river…

PAULINE: … not being caught on anything…

GREG: … would be virtually impossible.

PAULINE: He had trainers on… he never tied them up.

GREG: If he'd fallen in…

PAULINE: … he'd've kicked them off…

GREG: … instinctively.

PAULINE: And his woolly hat would have been washed up.

GREG: Everyone who's fallen into the Solent since Dan went missing has turned up…

PAULINE: … most the next day…

GREG: … they've all turned up.

PAULINE: Water temperature and fat content of a person determines how long it takes a body to come up…

GREG: If Dan hadn't got trapped, he should've turned up quickly.

PAULINE: Bits of headlamp were discovered in a field 3-400 metres away from the pontoon a few weeks after Dan went missing.

GREG: We're adamant that these were from the one Dan had on that night.

PAULINE: Why were they so far from the pontoon?

GREG & PAULINE: How come? *(Pause.)*

PAULINE: Twenty-one months after Dan's disappearance human remains were discovered…

GREG: … now positively identified as our Dan's…

PAULINE: … encased in two socks… and a DC trainer…

GREG: … at Chapman's Pool, a remote area in Swanage in Dorset…

PAULINE: … miles from where Dan went missing.

GREG: But how did they get there?

PAULINE: And why were his laces tied? Dan would never, as a skater boy, tie his laces up.

GREG & PAULINE: We suspect foul play.

PAULINE: The search for Dan may be over but the search for the truth surrounding Dan's death will continue.

Section 2

NOODLES AND OUT!

PAULINE: The 1st of January 2002 was "just another day"… but after all that's happened, I remember it so vividly.

(As the cast move into the live action the pace picks up.)

DAN: Mum?

PAULINE: Yeh.

DAN: Can I go fishing?

PAULINE: What time will you be back?

DAN: Twoish.

PAULINE: Ask your father.

DAN: Okay.

PAULINE: It was like I didn't want to have the responsibility of making that decision… I just delegated it… "Ask your father."

GREG: It's going to be a cold night…

DAN: I know…

GREG: They say it's going to be -4°!

DAN: And?

GREG: Really freezing.

DAN: But can I go… please?

GREG: What did Mum say?

DAN: She told me to ask you.

GREG: What time are you going to be back?

DAN: 2:30… at the latest.

GREG: Fine by me.

PAULINE: We've never had any problems with Dan being out late, he's trustworthy, with friends we know and the pontoon's well lit… but criticism did come back after he went missing:

ALL: *(Changing role.)* "Fancy them letting him out at that time of night!"

PAULINE: The lads had been going night fishing over the last year… we were cool with it… you can't keep your child tied to your apron strings all your life.

DAN: *(Reverting back and talking to* **GREG***.)* Can I take that bait we were going to use the other day?

GREG: Course you can.

PAULINE: Shall I put your dinner up for you?

DAN: I'll get something else.

PAULINE: It's roast.

DAN: Don't worry!

PAULINE: I had this sort of daydream the other day… Dan was at the door… and I didn't know what to do… I was thinking "Oh my God, who do I ring first to say that he's home?"… and Greg said:

GREG: Just bring him in and give him a cup of tea!

PAULINE: There's a big emptiness in our lives.

GREG: Some nipper came round this afternoon asking if you were doing another fishing competition.

DAN: Who was it?

GREG: Different from the one who came last week.

DAN: How old… did Pip know him?

GREG: Older, I think.

DAN: What did you say?

GREG: I said I wasn't sure… and what with exams and…

DAN: Dad…

GREG: I didn't know what to say…

DAN: If anyone else comes, get their name and address and tell 'em that there will be another one… soon… okay… it was a laugh, and it made me a bit of money.

GREG: Sorry.

PAULINE: *(Entering with Chocolate Truffle Cake.)* Dan… look…

DAN: What?

PAULINE: I'd got his favourite…

DAN & PAULINE: *(She holds it up for him to see.)* Tesco's Finest Chocolate Truffle Cake.

DAN: Can I have some now?

PAULINE: No you can't!

CLARE: *(Entering.)* He adored that chocolate thing…

DAN: Save some for when I come in tonight… please!

PAULINE: We did… *(She places it on a table SL)*… but he was never to have it.

(Pause.)

A few moments later Dan was sat on the couch with his dad on one side and Clare on the other…

GREG: He had two packs of… these noodley type things…

CLARE: Two great big packets!

PAULINE: Two huge great packets of…

ALL: Super Noodles.

GREG: Then the friends that he was going with came up the driveway…

PAULINE: Dan's lived in Hamble all his life. He'd known George since playschool and Joe and Thom since the middle of primary school. They'd played in the same football team… always together… regular fixtures and fittings in our house… up until Dan's disappearance. They all stood there in a little line by the back door… the four of them…

PAULINE & GREG: Dan, Joe, Thom, & George.

PAULINE: You know, they were just leaving and I said to them:

Now remember… there are weirdos about so keep your noses clean… and stick together.

GREG: That was the golden rule… the only reason they were allowed to go.

PAULINE & GREG: Stick together.

GREG: They were the last words she said to them.

DAN: See you! *(Making to leave.)* Don't forget to save me some of that chocolate cake, Mum.

PAULINE: He was such a good-natured boy… we never had any nastiness. At about eight o'clock he walked out, happy and smiling.
He knew how much he was loved and that means so much.
At least we have no regrets there.
I went to put some rubbish out and noticed the light was on in the garage. The door was half open and Dan was ducked down under it. He had his backpack on and was getting some bait from the freezer out there. I can remember… by the bins… it's strange… I really took that moment in. I don't know why… but I remember standing there just looking at our Dan.

CLARE: I heard the gate going and glanced out of the window… and there was Dan… always with his head down… always going fishing… carrying loads of stuff, I saw George take his bucket off him… like… to help. He had fishing rods, tripod stand and this bucket… this really big bucket.

(Pause.)

That was the last time I saw my brother. We were just starting to get close when he vanished… it was the worst timing.

PAULINE: And off they went, about a fifteen-minute steady walk. One was fifteen and the other three were coming up to fifteen and they were going fishing. They'd all been before, it was all so "normal".

Music 2: My Darling Child by Sinead O'Connor.

*(**DAN** repeats his departure in the manner described above… but in slow motion to the music. **PAULINE** and **CLARE** look on.)*

CLARE: They had actually planned this fishing trip two days earlier, on the 30th but Dan had been grounded so they couldn't go…

PAULINE: He'd been play fighting in the front room with his brothers…

*(**DAN** enters with his brother **LIAM**, setting up a brief series of images accompanied by loud overstated vocal reactions to establish the cushion fight.)*

CLARE: They were really going for it.

PAULINE: Things got a bit out of hand and…

DAN & BROTHER: *(They mime in slow motion trying to prevent the television being knocked over. They also speak in slow-motion voices.)* Smash… the… TV.

CLARE: The telly got knocked over.

PAULINE: Greg was furious.

*(**GREG** looks at **DAN** sternly. He could rant at him in a gobbledygook style language for comic effect.)*

CLARE: Dad made them all go out onto the back lawn and pick up the dog poo. *(**DAN** mimes picking up a piece as though with his hands.)*

PAULINE: *(To* **DAN***.) We did actually give them a pooperscooper thing.* **(DAN** *corrects his mime with a laugh.)* To look at them you wouldn't have thought it was punishment.

CLARE: They were all really laughing.

(The pace slows.)

GREG: His mates must have been really fed up with him when he was grounded, he messed up all their plans.

CLARE: Plans that none of us, at that time, were aware of.

GREG: We didn't detect anything out of the ordinary.

PAULINE: We just had our dinner, cleared up, then watched *Shakespeare in Love*. Clare went straight up to bed afterwards…

CLARE: … which was quite early for me.

Night, Mum.

PAULINE: Night.

Greg had gone up earlier 'cos he was due back at work after the New Year break.

I went to shut the computer off. It was half past eleven, I saw the clock on the computer.

I was sat in the corner and I had a real wrenching feeling in my tummy… like all of my insides being pulled out.

"Why am I feeling like this?" It was horrible.

I wanted to go down to the quay… I shook it off thinking…

"Pull yourself together, Pauline… you'd be such an embarrassment

for Dan". Then… I just fell asleep watching the telly.

CLARE: When Mum falls asleep I always come down and I say: "Mum, it's really uncomfortable down here… why don't you go to bed?" But she doesn't, she worries.

Music 3: Ave Maria *by* Jon Anderson.

Section 3

A MUCH LOVED SON AND BROTHER... DAN

*(Slides are shown during this section. The section should be underscored by the Adagio from **Handel's Water Music**.)*

Slide 1 – Dan as a baby[2].

PAULINE: Daniel was born on the 5th February 1987 weighing in at 9lb 12oz.

GREG: His easy-going nature was soon shown by regularly sleeping twelve hours straight, at the tender age of just six weeks.

PAULINE: This is Dan at two months, very bonnie baby, and already that smile everyone knows only too well, is developing. I wouldn't exactly say he's cute… more like a little chubby sumo I suppose!

Slide 2 – Dan with Bass.

This one shows Daniel when he's about five years old… holding up proudly his first Bass.

CLARE: A very big Bass.

GREG: He's holding it correctly with the fingers in the gills.

PAULINE: Again that smile's there and those dark eyes shining away. Daniel's a very keen fisherman… very keen.

He and his dad have a very, very special bonding between them over the fishing. Greg summed it up to me:

GREG: He's not just my son… he's my best mate.

Slide 3 – Dan and siblings.

PAULINE: Dan's the eldest of five. Eighteen months after Dan we had Clare, she's the only girl. Almost three years to the day we had Liam, the tiger of the family, then little Patrick came along, known to Dan and all of us as Pip. Then last, but certainly not least, and very much loved and…

CLARE: Cheeky one of the family… gets away with everything.

---

[2] The slides referred to in this and other scenes are available for use in performances of the play only. For details contact info@salamanderstreet.com.

PAULINE: Is little Conor. I'm so proud of our children, the way they've coped. I've told them Dan was a very special older brother and he loved them to bits.

Slide 4 – Dan with Saddam Hussein caption.

GREG: A local newspaper wrote an article about one of the searches, after Dan had gone missing.

PAULINE: Before we'd even seen it the newspaper concerned rang me up to apologise.

CLARE: Next to the article was a picture of Dan with the wrong name caption underneath.

Slide 5 – Close up of Dan with Saddam Hussein caption.

ALL 3: Saddam Hussein!

PAULINE: *(Laughing.)* Bless them, they were horrified but we just laughed. Dan would've really appreciated that but even then, when we laugh, there's an emptiness behind it. I can't replace Dan. The hole he's left in me. We have to be strong, but I can never be truly happy again.

CLARE: He loved the water… swimming, sailing, fishing, canoeing, Sea Scouts, and was several times local junior fisherman of the year…

PAULINE: …and he desperately wanted to join the Royal Navy… as an Officer.

Slide 6 – Navy letter.

GREG: Four months after he vanished he was offered a place at the Royal Navy College in Dartmouth for a potential Officers Acquaint course. I cried when I opened it. I was so proud of him but so sad he wasn't there to experience it.

Slide 7 – Dan's School Photograph 2001.

PAULINE: Dan's such a switched on kid… he was awarded a bursary into King Edward's School in Southampton.

GREG: He was involved in every possible club going from chess to football…

PAULINE: … and, well… so popular.

CLARE: He was really proud to be his team's top scorer for a couple of seasons.

GREG: He was the anchor to our family.

PAULINE: When he brought his school photograph home,
I remember I put it up against the first one he had done.
He'd grown into a young man.

(The Water Music continues, providing an aural bridge to the next section. **CLARE** *exits.* **PAULINE** *takes up a position away from* **GREG**.)

PAULINE: Greg… I was talking to this chap in Cowes today. *(Silence.) He lost his daughter. (Silence.) It's a frightening thought. (Silence.)* Greg… he told me that kids in Eastern European countries were being sold… sold for sex. Dan could have been abducted. He could have been down there and gone aboard a boat, or got in a car…

GREG: Pauline… don't…

PAULINE: We know that other teenage boys had been targeted… we know they were, so he could've been.

GREG: You're just upsetting yourself.

PAULINE: I want to figure out what happened.

GREG: I know.

PAULINE: And it… it could go on like this forever.

GREG: We've got to face it.

PAULINE: But you know what really upsets me… it's that no one was there with him. If someone had been there, it would almost certainly have reduced the chances of him being abducted. No one was there to raise the alarm. No one was there to witness if he had gone in the river. No one was there to help him. He was on his own. That was probably the first mistake he'd made… in his life.

GREG: He was such a good lad. I don't mean goodiegoodie, I mean...

PAULINE: I know exactly what you mean...

GREG: It's just not fair...

PAULINE: I want to... no, I... I need to know what he went through.

GREG: Pauline... there may never be a conclusion.

PAULINE: There's got to be.

GREG: We may never know what it is. That's what I can't accept... can't get to grips with.

(Silence.)

PAULINE: Why Dan? It doesn't seem real.

GREG: Life'll never be the same.

PAULINE: So many people walk such a fine line...

GREG: ... and they survive.

PAULINE: We've been privileged... blessed to've had a son like Dan...

GREG: Such a special boy, anyone who knew him will tell you that.

PAULINE: A very much-loved son... who has brought us so much joy
and laughter.

GREG: A son truly to be proud of.

PAULINE: We will always miss him.

GREG: We are missing him dreadfully.

(Pause. The cast silently position themselves for the next scene.)

Section 4

SARAH'S STORY AND THAT SCHOOL PHOTOGRAPH

PAULINE: Shortly after the news had broken that Dan had gone missing, I received a lovely letter[3] from the mother of a girl who knew him at school, saying how we've actually helped her daughter, Sarah *(SARAH enters wearing school blazer, as do the others in this scene)*, who was with Dan when that school photo was taken. It was the one we ended up using in the 'Missing' campaign.

SARAH: We went in one by one. They had a mirror just before you go through the curtain tab and I was looking at it. Dan and his mates were having a laugh… mocking us.

DAN: *(Overplayed with affected voice.)* Does my hair look okay?

MAX: *(Overplayed with affected voice.)* Does my make-up look okay?

DAN: *(Overplayed with affected voice.)* Oh, can I borrow some lippy?

SARAH: He was just making jokes… but my friend… she was having a fit about it!

LORNA: *(Suitably over the top.) I so wasn't ready!* They took the picture like this. *(She pulls a funny face and remains momentarily in a still image.)*

SARAH: A little while after that I was at my locker and just couldn't find my maths textbook. Dan was always last, and he was casually getting his stuff together; him so laid back and me frantically searching.

Oh, I'm going to get so told off! Dan, have you got your maths book?

DAN: Which? This one?

SARAH: Yeh.

DAN: Do you want to borrow mine?

[3] You can read a copy of the letter referred to in this scene on page 64.

SARAH: Please.

DAN: Fine. *(He gives the book to* **SARAH**.*)*

SARAH: On the final day of the Christmas term we were in this
hyper-small corridor at our lockers and everyone was coming
past us… *(***MAX** *enters.)* piling in.

*(***MAX** *is barged over by a friend.)*

Max, Dan's locker partner, actually got pushed onto the floor.
(They help **MAX** *up.)* We were all in hysterics. As people gradually
move off, you wish them a Happy Christmas.
I was the last one; talking to my friend. Dan was walking out
with Max and I just called out:
"Bye, Max. Bye, Dan."

MAX: See you.

DAN: Bye.

SARAH: I remember them saying…

MAX & DAN: Have a good Christmas.

(They exit in lively manner.)

SARAH: Yeh… you too!

It was just a little moment. *(Pause)* I wish I could have said
goodbye properly.

Music 4: Humpty Dumpty Love Song by Travis.

DAN *re-enters in slow motion to exchange Christmas cards with* **SARAH,**
*in a moment of privacy she wishes they had been able to have. Perhaps she
kisses him lightly as he leaves.*

Section 5

MISSING!

PAULINE: I woke up in the front room at about ten past two. Dan wouldn't want his mother sat on the couch waiting for him, so I went up to bed and waited, expecting to hear him come up the stairs, you know, typical teenager, then stick his head round the door to say he's caught something or whatever. He always let me know that he'd got home safely.

Come half two, quarter to three it hadn't happened. I was in bed looking at the digital clock and I said to Greg:

"Dan's not home yet." I'll never forget Greg's words…

"That's a bit cheeky." Not "that's unusual" but…

GREG: That's a bit cheeky, I thought they'd've been home earlier tonight 'cos it's so cold, -4° they said on the forecast!

PAULINE: I'm going to find out what's going on.

GREG: Pauline, are you sure?

PAULINE: He's not back!

GREG: He's probably round at one of his friends.

PAULINE: Now, Dan doesn't have a mobile.

GREG: We say to our kids that we'll get them a mobile, but they have to pay for the calls.

PAULINE: And although he's quite a little entrepreneur making quite a bit of money…

GREG: … he wouldn't spend it on phone calls.

PAULINE: I rang both his friends and got their answer phones. I didn't want to disturb their parents as it was… well, they had work in the morning. I'll go and check if everything's okay. *(She exits.)*

GREG: Do you want me to come?

PAULINE: No, I'll only be a moment.

GREG: *(Putting his shoes on.)* She was gone longer than I was expecting so I got dressed and began to feel a bit uncomfortable, just waiting for her to come back.

PAULINE: *(Running in.)* They're not there. Their stuff's all there, but they're not.

GREG: Are you sure?

PAULINE: Course I am.

GREG: They must be.

PAULINE: They've fallen in…

GREG: They can't have done…

PAULINE: They have. Their stuff's still there… on the pontoon.

GREG: What?

PAULINE: Dan's tripod stand was like collapsed in the corner, like he was packing it away then suddenly stopped or, I don't know… been stopped. One of them must have fallen in and then he probably tried to…

GREG: Pauline, love…

PAULINE: His backpack was… like it had just been chucked down. It was in the middle, you had to go round it to get to his other stuff. His gloves, they were there as well. It was spooky. What are we going to do?

GREG: He's probably round one of his friends.

PAULINE: But they wouldn't leave their stuff on the pontoon? It just doesn't make sense.

GREG: I'll go round to Thom's. *(To audience.)* Thom only lived two doors away.

PAULINE: What if they have fallen in, Greg?

GREG: I'll go round. If he's not there we'll call the police… but he will be. He's got to be…

PAULINE: What are you going to say to Andy? What if they have all fallen in? What are you going to say, Greg?

*(**PAULINE** and **GREG** move to an area representing **ANDY**'s house. They knock insistently and call his name… but with control over volume. **ANDY** enters wearing a dressing gown.)*

ANDY: *(Speaking loudly enough to be heard over the banging and calling.)* At four o'clock I was woken up with a panicky banging on the window. I had absolutely no idea who it was. Having heard Thom come home I thought it can't be to do with the boys. I went to the door. *(The banging stops. Silence.)* Pauline and Greg were stood there, and Pauline's words were:

PAULINE: The boys aren't back from fishing.

ANDY: *(Bleary eyed.)* My Thom's in.

GREG: Is our Dan there?

ANDY: No.

PAULINE: Can you check?

ANDY: He's not here.

PAULINE: Can we talk to Thom?

ANDY: Thom came out to the top of the stairs.

GREG: Do you know where Dan is?

THOM: *(Wearing a dressing gown.)* Isn't he at home?

PAULINE: No. He did come home with you, didn't he?

THOM: He was following us.

PAULINE: His stuff's still down on the pontoon.

THOM: He said he was coming up behind us.

GREG: Wasn't he with you then?

THOM: We just… I don't know. When I got in I saw him walking past, going up towards yours.

PAULINE: You're sure it was him?

THOM: Yeh, I am. Yeh.

PAULINE: Maybe Dan went back with Joe?

THOM: He didn't!

PAULINE: Are you sure?

THOM: Yes.

PAULINE: Right, I'm going to phone the police. *(Exits.)*

GREG: When did you get back?

ANDY: About midnight wasn't it?

THOM: *(Nods in affirmation.)* He was just behind us.

GREG: And you saw him going up our drive?

THOM: *(Long pause.)* I'm not sure.

ANDY: Thom, when did you last see Dan?

GREG: He came home with you… at midnight?

THOM: He wasn't with us exactly.

ANDY: You saw Dan going up his drive?

THOM: *(Pause.)* No.

GREG: *(Pause.)* You didn't?

THOM: *(Pause.)* No.

ANDY: What?

GREG: Where is he, Thom?

THOM: I don't know.

ANDY: Thom, did you see him or not? What happened?

THOM: *(Pause.)* He followed us home. I know he did.

GREG: This's looking serious, I'm going back to the pontoon. *(Exits.)*

ANDY: What do you want us to do?

(The action freezes momentarily.)

PAULINE: I phoned the police. I wasn't really panicking because I constantly expected him to walk in through the door. It was unreal but I had to get the ball rolling… to get everything going. They ask you questions… so many questions…

GREG: How old is he? What does he look like? Have you got any recent photographs?

PAULINE: By half past four all the emergency services were out on the water.

GREG: The helicopter, the local Hamble rescue, dogs, police, you name it, it was out there.

PAULINE: The initial response was brilliant. When I saw the divers in the water it made me feel sick. I thought they were going to pull Dan out.

GREG: If he had fallen in the chances were that he would be found sooner rather than later.

PAULINE: I remember going across to the shop about half six in the morning to get some milk. I just wanted to scream "I can't find Daniel!" It was a really eerie feeling because people were just getting on with their day to day lives… I was thinking "You're going to find out soon that our Dan's missing".

GREG: People heard it on the radio so we got loads of calls…

PAULINE: … but they thought it was Greg so I had to say, "No, it's Dan."

CLARE: I remember lying in bed hearing all the running around and stomping on the stairs and thinking, "Dan's in serious do-do's when he gets back." Mum was really worried about how to tell me and I said, "It's all right, Mum. I've heard everything. He'll be round at one of his friends." I never thought…

PAULINE: Later on down at the quay they were emptying the bins. I said: "You've got to check them first!" They did when I was standing there but after that… I don't know.

GREG: Twelve hours after Dan went missing we had a conversation with our first Police Liaison Officer.

*(Indicates **PLO**.)*

PAULINE: I was horrified. The conversation went something like this... as I remember it.

PLO: Did he take anything with him... clothes... money?

GREG: He's not taken anything!

PLO: The £600 you said he'd saved for his...

GREG: Already checked... it's still in his account.

PLO: I'm sorry to say this but... well, I really do think that you do have to accept that your son has slipped into the river.

PAULINE: Accept?

GREG: There's no proof whatsoever of anybody falling off the pontoon...

PAULINE: Is there any evidence?

PLO: No.

GREG: Who's saying this then?

PAULINE: Have you found anything at all?

PLO: Well, no.

PAULINE: He's missing, isn't he? You can't say he's drowned, he's missing. You're not looking for a stolen car. This is my son... my beautiful son. I'm not having assumptions made about him!

GREG: *(Comforting)* Paul.

PAULINE: He could be curled up in the undergrowth somewhere... and...

PLO: I'm sorry, Mrs Nolan.

GREG: *(To **PLO**.)* We've made a list of all the CCTV cameras in the area. Could you check them out for us?

PLO: Thanks.

PAULINE: They didn't even know some of those cameras were there!

GREG: It transpired that all of them were either broken or switched off!

PAULINE: *(Composing herself.)* We'll need posters.

PLO: I'll action that.

PAULINE: I'll get Dan's uncle on the case as well. He printed the missing posters.

Thank God I did. We had to wait a good week before we had any from the police.

GREG: When an under eighteen-year-old goes missing an official body should move in. There should be set procedures.

PAULINE: We assumed that the police would take us through every step…

GREG: … that Dan's face would be absolutely everywhere, appeals on national TV…

PAULINE: … and everyone would be aware… that all the wheels just click into place and get going.

GREG: But it's not like that. There's no set formula, it's up to the individual police force.

PAULINE: It was almost like we were swept under the carpet. We didn't know how to handle that…

GREG: … and we didn't know how to stop it.

PAULINE: We battled for thirteen months following Dan's disappearance before his case became a fully-fledged criminal investigation. It was so frustrating.

(Pause.)

GREG: But the response from the locals in Hamble was superb.

PAULINE: Dan loved his village and it was obvious they loved him.

GREG: Boys on bikes were knocking on the door and people took time off work to go out postering.

PAULINE: They were going everywhere.

GREG: Dan also loved his school, and Sarah, Dan's friend, tells how she reacted to the news of Dan's disappearance:

SARAH: I knew nothing about it until the afternoon of January the 2nd. Mum was driving me home from dancing. The news came on, it was a lady. She said something like,

A Hampshire boy has gone missing.

Then…

Daniel Nolan.

I felt like everything in my body had gone completely dead.
Back at school everyone tried hard to act normal, but it was…
you didn't know what to… you didn't… know what to say, like,
do you talk about him in the past or in the present? Some people
were saying he'd been drinking. No one had that image of Dan,
I was really surprised.

I've never heard the Crush Hall be so quiet for an assembly…
ever. Our priest said we must pray for his family. It was the
longest prayer we've ever had. There were a couple of sniffles
in the audience; I was crying, I'll admit that. A couple of people
had to walk out. The whole place was so sombre.

That maths book of Dan's that I borrowed… I've still got it.
It stays in my locker now, it's just a little memory of him,
I wouldn't want to lose that. People didn't like talking about
Dan while he was missing. They said it upset them. I found
that really depressing. It made me think that they were kind of
forgetting him.

I'll remember the little things, like him swinging on his chair
or doing homework in the group bases… which is forbidden…
because homework, as the teachers say, is for home.

I'll remember his sense of humour and his smile…

I'll remember him making me laugh.

I won't ever forget Dan Nolan.

Section 6

THE PONTOON

PAULINE: From what George, Joe and Thom said and what Detective Superintendent Andy Stewart, who was initially in charge of the investigation, has discovered, we've managed to piece together this version of what happened that evening:

*(**DAN** enters wearing the clothes he wore on that night, a beige Henri Lloyd jacket, blue cotton trousers and Air Force blue DCs with the laces untied. He is rushing about to collect his stuff together.))*

PAULINE: Now remember, there are weirdos about so keep your noses clean, and stick together.

DAN: *(Making to leave.) Don't forget to save me some of that chocolate cake Mum! (Re-entering with fishing equipment.)*

(Announcing his name to the audience) Dan!

THOM: Thom!

GEORGE: George!

JOE: And Joe!

ALL: Four boys... out for a night... and ready to... go!!! *(**GEORGE** runs off enthusiastically.)*

DAN, THOM & JOE: Not so fast, George!

GEORGE: Why?

JOE: We've got to get something.

GEORGE: What're you on about?

THOM: Put your hand in the bush!

GEORGE: Why?

DAN: Go on... just do it...

GEORGE: *(Bringing out a bottle of vodka.)* Vodka?

THOM: It's your lucky night, George. We were going to have it the night before last, then...

THOM & JOE: Dan got grounded.

DAN: Yeh, good one, eh?

GEORGE: It's been opened...

THOM: … and some bugger's nicked some…

JOE: Dan?

THOM: Couldn't you wait?

DAN: I didn't have much!

JOE: He'd drunk what would have filled the neck of the bottle.

THOM: Tonight's going to be a real laugh.

DAN: Maybe you'll actually catch a fish!

ALL 3: Tell us the secret of your rod, oh mighty one!

DAN: Shut up and put the drink in my backpack before anyone sees it.

Music 5: One Fine Day by The Offspring (plays loudly as the boys engage in a brief choreographed horseplay to establish the atmosphere of the fun they were having at that point in the evening, and to represent the journey to the pontoon.)

GEORGE: When we got down there we cast our rods out.

JOE: The tide was coming in.

THOM: It'd be high tide at twelve o'clock.

JOE: We were going to fish the tide in and then fish it out for a couple of hours.

THOM: I don't tend to catch a lot.

GEORGE, DAN & JOE: A lot? You never caught anything! *(DAN catches a fish.)*

THOM: Dan did all the time, don't ask me why.

GEORGE: Dan and Thom had brought some stuff down to eat. Joe hadn't eaten since two o'clock.

JOE: I wasn't really hungry.

THOM: Dan was drinking his milk.

GEORGE: And Thom was eating his nice cheesy Pringles.

JOE: We thought the vodka would help keep us warm. *(He swigs from the bottle.)*

GEORGE: I didn't have any.

OTHERS: Go on, George.

GEORGE: Don't want any.

> **JOE** *and* **THOM** *started messing around, being high, talking out loud. As the night went on they got a bit more giggly.*

THOM: Me and Joe were like…

JOE & THOM: *(Shouting from opposite sides of the stage.)* … shouting at one another…

THOM: … nothing in particular, just larking about. *(They come together.)*

GEORGE: They were falling on top of each other and acting as if they were drunk. One of them took some camouflage paint, green and black face paint, and put it on the other one.

JOE: Have some of this.

THOM: It's on my coat, you nonce!

DAN: *(With a fish on his line.)* Whoa! Look at this! What a beauty!

GEORGE: *(Looking in the opposite direction.)* Dan?

DAN: George, look! Brilliant, eh?

GEORGE: Who's that?

DAN: Who's what?

GEORGE: Him up there. Creepy or what?

DAN: George, what are you talking about?

GEORGE: He's like someone off Scooby-Doo.

DAN: Oh him!

GEORGE: Do you know him then?

DAN: The Gaffer.

GEORGE: The what?

DAN: The Gaffer. If we mess about he chucks us off.

GEORGE: Seriously?

DAN: Yeh.

GEORGE: What about them two then?

DAN: They're alright, unless they come down here.

GEORGE: How do you know him?

DAN: I was here just before Christmas and he came right down…

GEORGE: What did he do?

DAN: *(**DAN** runs round **GEORGE** and pretends to draw a huge knife on him, then suddenly stops in his tracks.)* Nothing!

*(He taps **GEORGE** on the head playfully.)*

GEORGE: He's creepy!

DAN: He's alright.

GEORGE: He hasn't got a face.

DAN: It's just 'cos the light's coming from behind him, you weirdo!

GEORGE: Who'd wear a cloak like that these days?

(Pause.)

DAN: Look it's ten, your dad'll be here in a moment.

GEORGE: I'm glad them two aren't here, don't know what he'd do if he saw them.

DAN: Dad's strict, isn't he?

(Silence.)

GEORGE: When I left I turned to Dan and said: *(With an affected humorous tone.)* See you later.

DAN: See you mate.

GEORGE: *(Slowly turning to the audience, slowing the pace.)* I left him there.

(Silence.)

Just the fact that I was there on that night when he vanished makes me think it was partly my fault. I could have told him to come home with me… I should have stayed so I'd've been with him… when they went home.

*(**GEORGE** exits.)*

THOM: We didn't see George's dad arrive but after a while we went back down and got on with our fishing. Dan'd caught three fish. We just sat there and talked, then Joe was sick… on the bridge.

THOM & DAN: Bloody hell, Joe!

DAN: Are you okay?

JOE: Does it look like it?

THOM: Why don't you lie down and try and get some kip?

JOE: *(Moving onto the bench.)* I feel… phew!!!

DAN: Thom, I'm off to get some chocolate.

THOM: Will it still be open?

DAN: Should be, it closes at eleven tonight.

THOM: Joe's virtually asleep. Is it alright if I come too?

DAN: *(To **JOE**.)* Will you be alright on your own?

THOM: We'll only be a minute.

JOE: Fine, whatever. What's the time?

THOM: Half ten.

DAN: Come on, Thom!

THOM: The shop was shut but then Dan saw some lads he knew at the bus stop and went over to talk to them. I was getting cold, so I went back down to Joe.

GREG: The lads at the bus stop told us that they asked Dan the time. He was able to read his analogue watch. It would appear from these comments that although he had been drinking, he was still capable and aware.

DSI STEWART: Shortly after this the boys at the bus stop, realising the bus was not coming, get up and walk off.

Daniel Nolan walks down the High Street, towards the pontoon. *(As though shouting out across the road.)* He calls out to a woman who is parking a car.

A party from the Bugle Pub walk up in the opposite direction. Another woman who knows Daniel drives down the High Street and sees him.

He walks to the top of the High Street and has a brief conversation with the Bugle party. His behaviour towards all of these witnesses leads the police to believe that Daniel Nolan was by any definition "drunk".

THOM: *(To **JOE** on the Pontoon. Waking him up.)* Joe… how are you feeling?

JOE: Shit

THOM: I'm freezing.

JOE: I'm not, must be the vodka!!!

THOM: What do you want to do then?

JOE: *(Sitting up)*. Where's Dan?

THOM: He's met some people he knows up at the bus stop.

JOE: *(As he moves he starts to retch.)* Oh God!

THOM: What?

JOE: How long's he going to be?

THOM: How do I know?

JOE: Thom… I've got to get home… I'm feeling like… *(He retches.)*

THOM: Let's pack our stuff up then.

JOE: It's so frigging cold.

THOM: A minute ago you said you weren't!

JOE: That was a minute ago! *(Struggling to pack his rod away.)* Oh my God!

THOM: Come here, I'll do that.

JOE: Thom… I… I think I'm going to throw up again. *(He retches.)*

DSI STEWART: Joe and Thom packed up their gear and walked up into the High Street. They met Daniel Nolan outside the Victory Pub.

JOE: My last image of Dan was coming down towards us. He seemed all right then. He could obviously hold his drink.

GREG: The facts of this last known sighting of our Dan, outside the Victory Pub in Hamble at about 11:40pm, were not established until four weeks after Dan's disappearance. At first, the police were told that this last sighting was on the bridge of the pontoon… placing Dan much nearer the water.

THOM: Dan, Joe's not feeling too good so I'm going to take him home.

DAN: I'll come back as well. Can you help me with my stuff?

THOM: I've got Joe's.

GREG: He only had his and Joe's rods tie wrapped together.

DAN: Okay.

THOM: All the time I was talking to Dan, Joe was walking on up the road… not very far but… I was like stuck in the middle.

DSI STEWART: Here were three boys, who had consumed a litre bottle of vodka, which was nearly full, and one other caffeine-type stimulant drink which would have increased the rush to the heart.

JOE: I was feeling really rough. I leant up against a window.

THOM: You could say that I made the wrong choice in deciding to take Joe home; I didn't know who to go with.

DSI STEWART: None of these boys were bad lads, just normal children.

THOM: I feel guilty about it 'cos I could have, like, gone down and helped Dan with his stuff.

(**THOM** *shows through his movement the dilemma he is in. He veers towards* **JOE** *but remains looking at* **DAN**. **GREG** *moves into his path.* **THOM**, *still looking towards* **DAN**, *bumps into* **GREG** *prompting him to stop speaking.* **THOM** *backs off a little.*)

GREG: It would only have taken a little while to go back down there and pack his stuff up…

THOM: *(Moving past* **GREG**, *but addressing him.)* I made that decision because I felt Joe was a lot worse off than Dan… and anyway… Dan seemed to agree with what I was doing.

JOE: I just wanted to get home. As soon as I stood up again I thought
I was going to be sick. *(Exits.)*

THOM: Dan said that he was going to follow us up.

DSI STEWART: Witnesses talked about Daniel Nolan swaying around discussing the quantity of alcohol he'd drunk. Even considering an element of male bravado it becomes clear that Daniel played a significant part in his own destiny on January 1st 2002.

GREG: The alarm that Dan had gone missing didn't go out for another four hours. Vital time was wasted, because Dan was on his own.

PAULINE: If three teenage girls had been out that evening and had been drinking I wonder if they would have become separated. Girls are taught from a very young age about their vulnerability and are more acutely aware of staying together.

GREG: A girl would be nervous of being on her own at night, whereas a boy possibly doesn't think anything of it.

THOM: When Dan first disappeared I was very shocked. I'm starting to realise we won't be able to do the things we used to do again, but I can't accept the fact that he's gone. It's more like he's on holiday or a school trip. There are so many things that I wish I could tell him… but I can't.

My dad wanted to… well… he just wanted to say something:

ANDY: As a parent you often wonder what your kids get up to when they are out on their own… but as kids go these four are probably the most reliable around, so the only requirement we made was they were back by 2.30 am. We never thought they would be taking alcohol with them, so to find that three of the four had shared a bottle of vodka neat(!) was more than a surprise.

I understand kids like to experiment with all sorts of things, including alcohol. Unfortunately this experiment went very wrong… wrong in many areas. Dan and Thom left Joe alone when they went to the shop. Thom and Joe then left Dan to collect his own fishing stuff. It was wrong. But it happened, in my opinion, because they'd polished off a bottle of vodka. How can we expect them to act normally after that? Without the vodka they always went together and came back together.

As I said before this was one experiment with tragic consequences.

I know our loss is not in the same league as Pauline and Greg's. It's not comparable… but… well… *(Hesitantly.)*… we can't avoid the feeling that… part of our Thom disappeared too… on New Year's Day 2002.

*(**PAULINE** and **GREG** move to the chocolate truffle cake and put a candle on it. **GREG** lights the candle.)*

PAULINE: I find myself feeling guilty if I enjoy myself… feeling guilty about getting into a warm bed… feeling guilty about having a hot meal. To have one of your children missing is so hard, but life goes on… no… time goes on… but for Greg and I… our lives are in suspension.

GREG: There are so many unanswered questions… so many ideas of what might have happened… But no evidence…

PAULINE: … no evidence whatsoever. There was a break-in at a second-hand clothing shop on the High Street.

GREG: The only opportunity for that to have happened was on that night… January 1st … the night Daniel went missing.

PAULINE: He was wearing a £200 Henri Lloyd sailing jacket.

GREG: Now, if someone's going to break into a second-hand clothing shop… *(A brutal [and very quick] murder on **DAN** is mimed.)*

PAULINE: What wouldn't people do for drug money?

GREG: Perhaps he saw something he shouldn't have seen.

PAULINE: We launched "Mateminders" on Dan's birthday the month after he disappeared, with the slogan:

ALL: Your mates matter. Stay together. Stay safe.

GREG: We want to find something constructive from what is every parent's worst nightmare.

PAULINE: All this has to have happened for a reason. Perhaps this is why…

GREG: We don't want anybody to feel how we are feeling.

PAULINE: We need to try and make a difference.

DAN: Drinking…

GREG: … smoking…

PAULINE: We've all done it, but if you do whatever it is together you will be able to experiment more safely.

DAN: Shut-up and put the drink in my backpack before anyone sees it.

PAULINE: The message we want to get across is to stay together all the time.

GREG: That was the golden rule… the only reason they were allowed out.

PAULINE: We can't keep our kids locked up. They have to go out and explore, but safety in numbers is the only way to go in this day and age.

GREG: Whether Dan chose to leave his friends, or they chose to leave him is irrelevant…

PAULINE: Now remember… there are weirdos about… keep your noses clean… and…

ALL: … stick together.

THOM: When we got to the cutway I looked back to see Dan but he wasn't there. I didn't think he'd be that far behind. Joe went off to where he lives and I went back home.

GREG: A taxi driver sighted Dan's two friends but not Dan, even though he was looking out for his fare!

The Nightwatchman, the one they call the Gaffer, said he saw Dan's two friends leave the pontoon and go up past him.

(All exit, leaving **PAULINE**, **GREG** *and* **DAN** *alone on stage.* **GREG** *continues the speech once they have left and there is stillness.)*

From where he was situated he should have had a good view of the pontoon. It was a very bright night, but our Dan was never sighted after Thom and Joe's departure.

PAULINE: It's very strange, very strange… but people don't just vanish into thin air.

Music 6: Silent Night *by* ***Sinead O'Connor*** *plays.*

PAULINE *extinguishes the candle. There is a slow motion movement sequence set to the music which* **PAULINE** *and* **GREG** *observe sadly showing* **DAN** *"disappearing". It remains unclear where he has gone.*

The Stage darkens.

THE END.

Deleted Scene

CONOR'S STORY

In the original play *Dan Nolan – Missing* there was a scene where Dan's youngest brother tried to make sense of his brother's disappearance. The story is so poignant that we have decided to include it in this version of the play as an Appendix.

PAULINE: I never dreamt in a million years that this far down the line I'd be no closer to finding him. It's been difficult for his brothers and sisters too… but… I've got to tell you this… Conor, Dan's little brother, has made up his own idea of what's happened. It really made me laugh. Last night he came down from his bed… he's going to kill me for saying this… he's decided that since Dan's been missing he's been in…

DAN: *(Drumming begins.)* Africa.

ACTOR 1: *(Somehow becoming the camel.)* On a camel.

ACTOR 2: *(Directing the camel with* **DAN** *on top.)* And he's slowly making his way back to England.

Slide 8 – School Photo Missing Poster.

PAULINE: However, when he got close to Hamble…

ACTOR 2: He became excruciatingly embarrassed by all of the publicity.

DAN: Aaaargh!!!

PAULINE: And he shrank…

ACTOR 1: … and he shrank…

ACTOR 2: … and he shrank…

PAULINE: … right down to a little person…

ALL: Ahhhh!

PAULINE: Just as he arrived at our house a…

ACTOR 1 & ACTOR 2: … great big giant came along…

PAULINE: … and frightened Dan!

DAN: Aaaaaargh!!!

ACTOR 1 & ACTOR 2: *(Proud of Power.)* So he turned and ran way.

DAN: 'Cos he was very, very frightened!

PAULINE: Conor believes he's somewhere on the grass verge on the Hamble Lane bend, just a few yards from our house.

DAN: He's waiting for a big gap in the traffic.

PAULINE: There's lots of cars on Hamble Lane.

ACTOR 1 & ACTOR 2: He's got a mighty long wait!

DAN: And when he thinks that there's about half an hour without any traffic…

ACTOR 2: He'll cross the road!!!

DAN, ACTOR 1 & ACTOR 2: And make his way to our house.

PAULINE: When he gets within the four walls of our house, Conor has informed me, he will grow back into his big size and he'll be fine then when he's inside. So I'll go along with that. I'm quite happy to go along with that.

GREG: The children think about it and so do we. It's with us twenty-four seven.

A Challenge for Students Exploring
Missing Dan Nolan from Mark Wheeller

A nice little challenge would be for a group of four to stage the Reflections of the Original OYT Cast *as a documentary play with the specific task to add as much viable movement as possible to make it visually interesting.*

This is the kind of exercise I would do with my students to introduce them to the play for these reasons.

1. They will experience what the cast of OYT went through in attempting to put Missing Dan Nolan *onto stage… it's not easy… there are no obvious answers… they have to be worked at and invented.*

2. This is exactly what verbatim/documentary theatre is… words that were written (or in the case of verbatim, spoken) to tell a story. They aren't natural dialogue such as you'd find in a traditional play.

3. The challenge of a performing group is to be imaginative with the presentation to ensure that it is visually arresting as well as verbally interesting. It should come across to the audience as though these works were naturally at home on stage.

4. There is no better way to ensure that students really take the material in and understand it as they 'become' the characters.

5. When they read Missing Dan Nolan *after staging this "scene" they will have a far better grasp of how to approach the staging of that play (and any other one in a similar style) and that play will be easier as it has so much more emotional content and implied movement.*

Reflections of the Original OYT Cast
Documentary Theatre style (2020)

Edited by Mark Wheeller from the written memories of Rachael Dennett (Clare), Darren Harley (Dan), Kate Berwick/was Dean (Pauline) & Alex Chalk (Greg).

RACHAEL: Oh my goodness, reading the introduction Mark has written for this new script, has given me goosebumps, taking me back to feeling fifteen/sixteen again and being confronted with this mammoth task of doing justice for this hugely important play, which was THE MOST important thing I'd ever been involved in and, at times, it exceeded the importance of my GCSE exams but it also gave me an excitement I'd never experienced before.

DARREN: It only seems like yesterday we were performing the play. I remember being in the theatre and Mark coming up to us, saying he had a project he would like us to help him with. All this, just as we had finished our GCSE drama exam!

KATE: For me, it was more than a production, it was a defining period in my teenage years. I was painfully shy when I joined Oaklands Youth Theatre. Prior to this, I had only ever been a very small part of other productions. Mark took a chance on me for this role and I will forever be grateful to have been involved in such an important project.

ALEX: The original idea was to put together a small piece, similar to an advert, to raise awareness. Little did we know how much this would change and the help we were able to offer this poor family in turmoil.

KATE: We didn't agree to be part of this lightly, we had a purpose, we needed to be as successful as we could be in raising awareness of the case of a real missing teenager. Newspaper articles and TV news features were a strange element of the process, but it was an amazing tool for us to utilise. The more we could get people talking, the more chance someone might remember something that could help.

ALEX: To begin with, Mark took the four of us to the National Theatre in London to see *Frozen* by Bryony Lavery with Anita Dobson, a play about a mother who lost her daughter. On the train on the way home we all reflected on how horrible it must be to go through something like that. As a teenager I could not fully relate but looking back at it now, as a parent myself, it is a premise that is simply heartbreaking. (It was on this train ride that we found out about Rachael Dennett's fear of feet!)

DARREN: I remember us all going to Hamble to have a look round. Walking from the car park opposite the shop down past the pub to the waterfront.

ALEX: We saw the pier where Dan had been fishing and this was in the black of night to capture the atmosphere. This is, to date, the most harrowing experience of my life. To think that someone of a similar age to me had been out with friends and was then never seen again. Horrible to think that can and, unfortunately does, happen to anybody. The secondary point of the play became very clear. STICK TOGETHER!!!

RACHAEL: This phrase…

ALL FOUR: Stick together!

RACHAEL: … which my friends and I have fond memories of, was similar to a tagline of our head teacher at the time 'Look after each other'. The two phrases have stuck with me to this day.

KATE: My involvement was coupled with some controversy. My family didn't fully appreciate the purpose of the project at first and felt it was in bad taste. I could understand their view; what clout could school children possibly have over current events? Thankfully, once they saw the early version, the support it had from Dan's family and the media interest, they realised just how much we were achieving.

RACHAEL: My family and I would often head down to Hamble before, during and after the rehearsals for the play as we lived locally and enjoyed spending time by the sea. We walked around the area and discussed what we thought might have happened that night, based on the facts and opinions we were presented with by being involved in the play.

The subject matter was hugely important to my family and, being part of this play, forced us to have some honest and scary conversations, sometimes linked to Dan's disappearance and staying safe.

ALEX: Initial preparations began with rehearsals on a Sunday evening at Oaklands Community School Theatre, the place where OYT spent so many hours. Mark encouraged young people to collaborate on different plays. Collaboration – Mark's ethos. Everyone as important as each other and no idea too silly or convoluted, 'let's try it and see how it goes.'

RACHAEL: Mark involved us creatively, asking us for our ideas and how things felt when we had run through them a few times.

Although rehearsals were hard work, I didn't mind because I knew the play was powerful and had to be told in the right way. I definitely wouldn't have had as much passion or commitment if this was a huge scale musical with a simple purpose; to entertain.

ALEX: Mark had the start of a script for us to work with which became an ever-evolving narrative that changed frequently and sometimes only hours before a performance!

RACHAEL: Rehearsals were long and sometimes exhausting. I remember one particular rehearsal where I had to work for what seemed like five hours on the movement for one of Clare's monologues. We knew we were in danger of creating a very static play, relying too heavily on the words to carry the drama.

Through rehearsals we found that often a simple movement using the stage blocks or repositioning the actor on the stage worked to ignite the imagination of the audience. I'm a drama teacher now and, in rehearsals with my own drama students, I use the example of Sarah (who I also played) and the locker, referring to this as 'the point of reference'. Mark asked me to visualise the locker behind me in the space so this became my 'point of reference' for this monologue. I created a 'relationship' with this object which gave me a sense of area to work with in terms of proxemics. This also helped the audience to 'see' a sense of space changing with the way that I interacted with the various different points of reference. This is so important for me now as a teacher because my students often have small spaces or limited sets to work with. We use this technique to explore how the character is feeling towards this point of reference which can be an easy way for students to start thinking about movement.

KATE: Playing a mother in such an unbearable situation, when I was only a teenager myself, was a huge responsibility. Making sure Pauline's message was heard, her desperation was felt and their family bond was portrayed, proved a delicate balance to reach.

I also had many monologues to deliver as Pauline. These are tricky to deliver at the best of times, so, here are some thoughts which helped me to achieve this as well as I could in my performance.

• Explore the mix of emotions involved and be mindful, avoid making a caricature from a real-life experience.

• Diction and subtlety was fundamental with our characters, especially in those key moments.

• With these large sections of script needing such stillness in the delivery, we were aware of the need to add interest and depth to the performance physically – techniques such as freeze frames, slow motion and imaginative lighting helped us draw the audience in to the moment.

• Our set was very simple. Blocks, a large missing poster and printed T-shirts that mirrored the original poster of the Missing Dan Nolan campaign. It was deliberately simple but chosen carefully to be a constant reminder of why we were there, to keep the audience focused on the real Dan and not our 'performance'. Simple, but effective.

RACHAEL: Diction and pronunciation for the actors is always key to ensure the audience understands the character's motivation and meaning, and now, as a drama teacher, I regularly get students to work on their vocal techniques, quality and clarity. Techniques such as 'actioning the script' (as I call it) to find the emotion and motivation is helpful before students tackle the vocal delivery.

ALEX: As a young person, just beginning college, I remember at points feeling I could not do it. I was playing Dan's dad – and yet I was a kid with no children of my own, so how could I relate and do this part justice? How could I show the true emotion of a father, helpless at the disappearance of his first born? This was compounded with the fact the he would be watching me – playing him. I felt like I was intruding, what right did I have to represent this man that I had not known previously with such a tragic topic? The fact remained – we were invested in this and there was no way I was turning back. The desire to help overwhelmed all others.

That said, I feel this was the production where I acted for the first time. Previously, I had performed in plays with a huge comedy element. This was easy for me, I never felt I had to try, as clowning had always been my forte. It was the reason I got involved in OYT in the first place – to expel the natural energy I had to be silly in a productive way and not in a classroom (although it is a characteristic of mine that still hasn't changed!).

I learnt fast, that to act was more than being silly in front of your friends. It's about investment in a role, understanding the part you are playing and fully embedding yourself into it. I would not go as far as to say that I was method acting, whenever I left the stage I quickly became myself again, but I found some of its teachings very valuable.

I also tried to impart humour into the play, (not always intentionally during the rehearsal process) and, it seemed to work. With a play this hard hitting, I felt the audience needed a respite and, what better way than through comedy?

Theatrically, I felt it added the perfect juxtaposition of pain and laughter. We needed it in the rehearsal process as it was so easy to get bogged down in the natural emotion of the piece.

DARREN: I remember the day we ended up in A&E because I broke my finger running around. I bet people thought we were mad rehearsing in the waiting room but later that afternoon we were due to perform it to his parents. I remember that very well!

RACHAEL: The most memorable rehearsals for me, by FAR, were performing for Dan's family and friends (cue the goose bumps again). We felt we had such a mammoth task. We didn't take this lightly and were fully focused to ensure we got it 'right'. Whilst performing and looking out into the huge theatre with its tiered seating and seeing empty seats, except for the small gathering of family members all together, was intense. It felt like a thousand eyes on us. This was more pressure than performing to a full auditorium, so when that happened it was so much easier.

KATE: The responsibility was huge. These were the people we were playing, telling their story, and serving as a reminder of the dreadful night that initiated the most difficult period in their lives. They could not have been more supportive. Their strength of character and love for Dan was contagious.

DARREN: Henri Lloyd were so good, giving me a coat . I still had it some ten years later!

KATE: During the long period (nearly two years) of rehearsals, shows and festivals there was barely a run of performances that could have been considered to be the same. Not only was the script fluid, our skills and performance choices were constantly evolving with the experience we gained and from the feedback we were given. I especially remember one performance where we were given a significant adaptation of our lines hours before we went on stage because there had been a tragic development in the news about Dan which we had to incorporate!

DARREN: Going to Daniel's school, King Edward's, for me was the strangest. Going in and performing in front of his friends.

RACHAEL: We performed in their intimate theatre, which was in the round, which was an added challenge for us as we'd always done it end-on. Performing to school-age children who knew Dan and his family was particularly difficult and we experienced a huge emotional response from them.

Later, I went on to make a friend (we're still good friends to this day) who went to King Edward's and recognised me from the play haha! That would have been five years after the show too! Random!

DARREN: I remember going to the festivals. The one that sticks out was Woking, where we won the Best Youth Production. As well as playing Dan I had the extra responsibility of going up with Danny (Sturrock) to sort out lighting and sound.

RACHAEL: I remember taking the performance to our first festival (Totton Drama Festival) and being slated. That was hard to take. When we were in our little bubble in the theatre you think you can rule the world and to be knocked back was hard to experience at that age. Mark's determination to continue (and support for the cast) made us realise not to give up and the project was worth fighting for, which it was :-)

This made winning at the bigger, Woking Festival all the more sweet, as we worked our butts off to improve and tweak an already, in our eyes, fantastic production.

ALEX: Throughout our time performing at various drama festivals, we became rather acclaimed. We had a hard-hitting piece that kept audiences of all ages at the edge of their emotional limits, often with the clear sounds of sobs coming from the audience – and (after Totton, when we sorted out our diction), it was a huge success. We celebrated. We brought hope (if only to ourselves) that maybe we could be the breakthrough in Dan being found, that the pain and suffering of the Nolan family could finally come to an end. Tragically, that wasn't to be, although while we were working on the play there was some closure for the family… but no celebrations.

KATE: We were humbled to be invited to perform a scene at a memorial service held for Dan to commemorate his disappearance. The family had total trust in Mark's work as a playwright, and asked us to share our efforts with the members of Dan's community. This was an incredible honour. We chose to share the scene where Connor tells his story about how Dan had gone missing and might possibly return safely. (This scene appears on page 61 of this script and works beautifully as a stand-alone scene.) It was the one time Connor, who was very young, was able to see any of the play. It was lovely to see him smile.

DARREN: Every time I hear the last song in the play (which was one Dan's mum told us he listened to), 'Wherever You Will Go' by The Calling, I am taken back and reminded of Dan and that whole time.

ALEX: As you will soon see, when you read the play, the conclusion for the family was far from the conclusion we all hoped for. But it was a conclusion and this again changed our play. (I call it ours as it belonged to all of us – us, Dan's family and friends, our own families and friends and anyone who saw it.)

The point I am trying to make is be prepared to adapt. Theatre is supposed to evolve, the first performance should not be the same as the last performance. Invest. Make it real. Real does not look the same from day to day.

Working on *Missing Dan Nolan* shaped elements of my life for years to come. I worked professionally for two different touring theatre companies over three years and loved every minute of it. I also worked for a theatre company as an acting coach for Key Stage 1, 2, and 3 children. Drama was my life!!

Follow your passion, if you want to succeed then it is more than possible. If a silly class clown like me can do it then you are more than capable!

DARREN: I remember going somewhere with Mark later on, to watch another group perform. I remember what a wonderful time it was to be helping a local family and what a pleasure it was to work with an amazing cast and crew.

RACHAEL: I had only recently joined Oaklands Youth Theatre (I was in Year 9 at this point the other three were all older) and I was enamoured by their talent and confidence. I was excited to become 'like them' and wanted my picture on the 'hall of fame' (the pictures of OYT plays in the entrance to our school (Oaklands) Theatre and to be a part of something big. Little did I know HOW big this opportunity would become and perhaps started my journey to becoming a drama teacher myself.

KATE: My time with OYT and with the amazing cast and crew of *Missing Dan Nolan* has undoubtedly shaped who I am. I might not have continued with drama professionally, but the confidence and skills I developed at a young age have carried me through my years in education and into a customer/client facing career that I am very proud of.

To this day I love the theatre. I spent several years as part of an amateur dramatics group and I now am lucky enough to have three children who, so far, love going to the theatre just as much as me.

ALEX: To wrap up I would like to offer this advice for when you are working on this script – work together and STICK TOGETHER. Don't be afraid to cry, to laugh, to shout. Support each other. Hug each other. Bring yourself fully to it and remember that people are watching and you are in a privileged position – you can continue the Nolans' hope that their message continues to spread and that no one else need go through what they went through.

Thanks for hearing us out and good luck!!!

A Note on the Original Lighting Design

The idea behind the lighting design for OYT's Production of the then-titled *Dan Nolan – Missing* came from a trip myself and Mark made with the cast to the Pontoon in Hamble after a rehearsal. This was a very strange experience for all involved and we were somehow nervous about being in the very place where Dan went missing. Standing on the pontoon and seeing various things that were mentioned in the play made it all very real and you couldn't but help to imagine what might have happened.

We had visited at night and the Pontoon was dimly lit. I recall a red light fixed on top of a pole sticking out of the water next to the pontoon. The water was calm with the light reflecting off of it. I could imagine the moonlight reflecting off of the water onto the lads while they were fishing that night. I wanted to replicate this in the opening scene of the play and opted to use two floor lights with steel blue glues and set these at 45 degree angles to light the faces of the characters. In addition I added a single white open spotlight shining down onto the pontoon to symbolise the moonlight.

The use of colour and the angles of the floor lights created a stillness and produced some great shadows of the boys fishing. As the opening music changed from a sombre version of 'Silent Night', highlighted by a siren sound effect and into the up tempo 'All The Small Things', I used the light at the pontoon as my inspiration and flooded the scene with red light, symbolising a warning of things to come in the same way that that single red light at the pontoon served as a warning of and obstruction in the water.

The lighting was very simplistic – but I think that is why it was so effective.

Danny Sturrock

Woking Drama Festival 2003

Dan Nolan – Missing by Mark Wheeller

Oaklands Youth Theatre
Adjudicated by Paul Fowler GODA

I have long been an admirer of Mark Wheeller's issue-led plays... there is an immediacy and theatrical brio about his writing that gives his subjects an instant efficacy. I know of no other playwright in Britain working in this way, addressing important issues in a manner that is so immediately relevant and accessible to both cast members and audience... Heart-rending, bold, direct and simple... even on the bare page this is a powerful piece of drama. This is more than documentary drama – it is also campaigning theatre at its most powerful.

If anything positive can be said to have come out of the awful tragedy of Dan Nolan's disappearance and death, then it is the knowledge that this play should serve as a lasting, and fitting memorial to Dan.

The eerie, dreamlike entrance in the wintry blue light to the haunting strains of Silent Night set exactly the right mood of that fateful New Year's Day before the atmosphere was expertly turned with crashing chords of Blink 182 accompanying the boys as they head banged, drank and vomited, before the effortless segue into the sibling argument that moved the scene deftly into the domestic.

Disciplined, committed and highly focused work.

I liked and admired much about this inventive, imaginative production – this is a director with great vision and marvellous control of pace and mood. The swift transformation from schoolboy roustabout to the poignant scene in which Sarah says the goodbye in her mind that she was denied in reality, was a great example.

I loved the way in which you developed a sort of choral punctuation with two or more actors emphasising a word or phrase, and the way in which this was echoed by a very different sort of punctuation from the two on-stage drummers.

Fabulous physicality… immaculate teamwork… exemplary.

Dan: This was a highly impressive performance that you rightly elected to play without sentimentality… terrific physicality, solid stage presence and great attack… a pleasure to see an actor so secure in the material… pick up was rapid as quicksilver. This was an immensely attractive, likable and above all truthful performance.

Pauline: The anguish of the distraught mother was portrayed with a direct simplicity and judgement that was just great. The despairing yet hopeful yearning you conveyed was very moving.

Greg: You played Dan's father with an air of authority far beyond your years, this was a performance of great truth and complete sincerity and highly effective as a consequence. The sequences as one of Dan's mates in the ill-fated fishing party were excellent, especially in the moments when you described how you left the pontoon.

Clare: I thought you were absolutely right and completely convincing as the sister who never realised quite how much she loved Dan until he was gone. Your two long speeches as Sarah were particularly impressive as you shared her memories of the friend she was never able to properly say goodbye to. The sadness and sense of personal loss was beautifully conveyed.

Vibrant, committed, unsentimental and truthful… teamwork one always hopes for but sees all too rarely!

The individual performances were first class and the direction showed the same flair, imagination and rigorous discipline as the writing.

Very Well Done Oaklands Youth Theatre, deserved winners of the Youth Award.

Paul Fowler GODA
(Adjudicator at The Woking Drama Festival 2003)

Woking Drama Festival 2003 – Adjudicator's Review – by kind permission from Paul Fowler GODA.

A Letter from Sarah's Mum

Dear Mrs Nolan,

A few lines to thank you so much for sending the poster of Dan. I now have it in the rear window of my car and pray that it will do some good.

As a mother of two teenage girls I can only imagine the torment and grief you must be experiencing, but I have to tell you we so admire your courage and positive attitude which inspires us to stay positive too.

Sarah had a very bad time during the first week and on her initial return to school, where I understand she sobbed throughout the first assembly. Now, thankfully, although she still hangs on every word of the news programmes and scans the *Echo*, as we all do daily, she has managed to adopt a more positive attitude, which is much easier to deal with, and talks of when he comes back to school.

I hope it will be of some comfort to you to know that like many, many others we pray daily for Dan's safe return and also that you and all of your family are given strength to carry on.

Until that brighter day dawns, our love and best wishes to you all.

Sarah's Mum

A Prayer from the 'Service of Hope', 1st January 2003

Where are you, Dan?

The beautiful baby boy with big dark eyes.

Who laid in my arms, when just a few hours old.

We watched you grow; a toddler, a little boy, and then onto school.

New friends, new interests, new skills, new sport; which you love so much.

All these things which helped you grow, to the maturing lad
we all now know.

Working in your special quiet way towards your ambitions,
goals and making dreams.

Where are you, Dan?

Oh Lord, we pray, please help him find his way back home to us, family and friends who love and miss him so.

Amen.

Nanny Bett (Dan's grandmother)

Digital Resources for Teachers

There are a number of practical digital resources for teachers and students who are studying *Missing Dan Nolan* as a set text.

The OCR has produced a Teacher's Guide for GCSE (9-1) Drama which is freely available on the internet for download.

https://www.ocr.org.uk/Images/284847-missing-dan-nolan-teacher-guide.pdf

The slides of Dan Nolan mentioned on p.39 are available for use in performances – please email info@salamanderstreet.com to discuss a licence for their usage.

Video recordings (and an interview with Mark Wheeller) of *Missing Dan Nolan* are also available for download – please see the *Missing Dan Nolan* page on www.salamanderstreet.com for further details.

Missing Dan Nolan DVD/Download

The DVD includes:

Two productions.

The original OYT production, directed by Mark Wheeller, with a cast of four as it prepared for the first TiE tour.

The Lichfield Garrick Youth Theatre large cast production, directed by Tim Ford in 2016.

Bonus Features:

Interview with Mark Wheeller

Available from Salamander Street.

Teachers – if you are interested in buying a set of texts for your class please email info@salamanderstreet.com – we would be happy to discuss discounts and keep you up to date with our latest publications and study guides.

Chequered Flags to Chequered Futures
Paperback 9781913630355
eBook 9781913630348

Chicken!
Paperback 9781913630331
eBook 9781913630324

Game Over
Paperback 9781913630263
eBook 9781913630270

Hard to Swallow
Paperback 9781913630249
eBook 9781913630256

Too Much Punch For Judy
Paperback 9781913630300
eBook 9781913630317

Hard to Swallow, Easy to Digest
(with Karen Latto)
Paperback 9781913630409
eBook 9781913630393

Hard to Swallow, Easy to Digest: Student Workbook
Paperback 9781913630416
eBook 9781913630423

The Story Behind … Too Much Punch for Judy
Paperback 9781913630379
eBook 9781913630386

Salamander Street will be publishing new editions of Mark's plays in 2020 – follow us on Twitter or Facebook or visit our website for the latest news.

www.salamanderstreet.com

CPSIA information can be obtained
at www.ICGtesting.com
Printed in the USA
JSHW020949160523
41628JS00001BA/1